5

Reasons
I'm Grateful
I Raise Support

Richard Malm

To Kathy -
We are also
grateful for wonderful
friends like you and Wes who
have encouraged and inspired us over the years.
Rick
& Jana

ORE
Publishing

Richard Malm c/o Ore Publishing
P.O. Box 291002
Kerrville, TX 78029-1002

Book Layout © BookDesignTemplates.com

Ordering Information for books by Richard Malm
www.bit.ly/amazonrickmalm

Five Reasons I'm Grateful / Richard Malm. —1st ed.
ISBN 978-0-9985085-1-1

Contents

Dedicated to the One
"who supplies seed to the sower
and bread for food
and will also supply and increase
your store of seed
and will enlarge the harvest
of your righteousness."

2 Corinthians 9:10

It All Started While Washing Dishes

I was standing at the sink washing dishes when I noticed a postcard on the window sill in front of me. It was from a missionary couple we support. They were thanking us for our financial partnership with their ministry.

Though we raise support ourselves we also support many other missionaries. In fact, most missionaries I know, support other missionaries.

Rather mindlessly I thought, "I'm so glad they raise support because otherwise we probably would have lost touch with them."

That thought reminded me of all the wonderful folks we stay in touch with through our own support raising efforts. As images and names of specific people on our support team flashed through my mind, I realized we would have never met many of these folks if we didn't raise support. In my head I heard myself saying, "I'm really grateful we raise support, too."

Those words shocked me back to reality. "What?! Did I just say, 'I'm grateful we raise support?' I think I did."

Again, pictures of some of the wonderful folks on our support team came to mind and I realized, "I **am** grateful we raise support. It has allowed us to meet so many special friends."

As I rinsed the next plate, I thought of amazing stories of God's provision - just the amount we needed at just the right time, strange ways we met some of our donors and even donors we've never met but who faithfully give to our ministry.

"Wow. So many incredible stories. I am so grateful we raise support."

As I finished the last pot, I thought, "I need to share these reasons for gratitude with our Commission To Every Nation missionaries and staff who raise their support. It's too easy to see support raising as a 'necessary evil' and not the great blessing it is."

Up From The Suds It Arose

I could see the title of a small book rising out of the soapy dishwater - *5 Reasons I'm Grateful I Raise*

Support. It was brilliant – probably divinely inspired. But the only problem was, so far, I only had two reasons - the amazing friends and the amazing stories we have because of it.

Even if there were no other reasons, those two would justify remaining continually grateful. But, over the next few weeks, as this idea rattled around in my head, I realized I have many reasons to be grateful God has chosen to provide for me and my family through the generous obedience of His people.

Because you're reading this I assume you, too, are either a support raiser, a supporter of others, or both.

If you're a support raiser, I hope this book will encourage you to stay locked in an "attitude of gratitude." You've been granted a sacred privilege of partnering with the Lord and His people to fulfill a dream. It's a dream God deposited in your heart and that He is diligently working through you to fulfill.

In the Old Testament, there were actually thirteen tribes of Israel but the Levites were never counted among the people. God said they were set apart and belonged to Him.

Like you, the Levites were granted the special privilege of being totally dependent upon the Lord and His people for support. They were given no land to work but were to fully serve in the Lord's work and He promised to care for them.

Modern support raisers follow in the tradition of the Levites – fully given to the Lord's work and fully dependent upon Him to provide for them, their families and the ministry needs.

If you support others, I hope this book will give you a tiny behind the scenes glimpse into how much your partnership - not just your gift - means to those you help. Your friendship and the confidence you express through your giving is a wonderful encouragement.

Rick Malm

Founder/President
Commission To Every Nation
Commission Ministers Network
2018

The Missionary Millionaire

Financially, I have almost nothing to show
for my forty-four years of labor
on behalf of the Indians.

We own an automobile
that you folks gave us two years ago,
a home in the jungles of Peru,
five hundred dollars in savings
for the education of children
and that's all.

In the wealth of friendship, however,
we are millionaires.

- William Cameron Townsend -
Founder
Wycliffe Bible Translators

Is Asking Legit?

At the moment I have all I need – and more! I am generously supplied with the gifts you sent me with Epaphroditus. They are a sweet-smelling sacrifice that is acceptable and pleasing to God. And this same God who takes care of me will supply all your needs from his glorious riches, which have been given to us in Christ Jesus.

Philippians 4:18-19

I Want To Be Like George

I got sucker punched at a prayer meeting. It happened at one of the first presentations I made when I initially raised support to go on the mission field.

Complete with indigenous handicrafts and colorful slides I told the small circle of attendees how we were going to Guatemala. I told them of the needs of the people and our need for financial supporters who would make it possible for us to go.

"We can't help them unless friends here help us. Please pray about supporting our ministry to Guatemala."

After some testimonies and a prayer time, the cookies came out. While standing at the refreshments table a couple approached me and punched me right in the gut. Not literally, but it sure felt like they did.

I had just spent 45 minutes passionately "spilling my guts." It was humbling - no, it was actually humiliating - to have to make our needs known and ask everyone to help us financially.

Then this couple cornered me by the coffee and introduced themselves with these thoughtful words, "We are missionaries, too. But we're like George Mueller, we don't make our needs known. We trust God."

Oooof! Nice to meet you, too.

Though I'd never met this couple, I'd heard about them. They were retired, lived nearby and their "missions work" consisted of occasionally driving a few hours south, crossing the border into Mexico and helping out for a few days or weeks before driving back home.

I'm sure they were making a difference but I was moving a young family of five to live full-time in a country in Central America that was embroiled in a brutal civil war. Not quite an equal comparison.

Several clever but unchristian responses came to mind. I managed to just smile and pretend it was nice to meet them.

But, while driving home I had a passionate discussion with the Lord. "God this is humiliating! I hate asking for support! Why can't I be like them? Why can't I just ask You and You take care of our needs?"

As I drove on through the dark I heard a soft response in my heart. It went something like this: "I want you to ask others because it **is** humbling and humility is good. It's only humiliating if you have pride inside. If I met your needs without you asking others, your pride would be out of control. You'd be totally arrogant - just like them."

OK, maybe I added the "just like them" part. But if the Lord didn't actually say it, I'm sure He was thinking it.

So, as much as I wanted to be the next George Mueller, just praying and trusting God, I found the Lord had a different plan for me. I had to pray, trust God and make my needs known to others.

It's Not Either / Or

I don't know where we get this silly idea that we either pray and trust God or we share our needs with others. As missionaries, making our needs known to others doesn't replace praying and trusting God. It's part of the "trusting God" process.

We pray, trust God and invite others to share in the joy of seeing God provide and accomplish His will through our living and giving.

In the particular church stream where I swim there's an assumption that not sharing your needs is more virtuous - a badge of spirituality. For many years, I labored under the same misguided delusion.

Then I had a revelation. While it sounds very spiritual to say, "I just pray and trust God," that method is actually much more appealing to my old carnal nature. I would love to just pray and trust God. I would love to not have to make my needs known to others.

In fact, if given a choice, every missionary I know would vote for the "just tell God" method. "Just pray" and "just tell God" is "just perfect" as far as my old ego goes.

It's hard to ask. It's humbling to ask. I would prefer to keep it between me and God. My vanity would never be confronted. In fact, as I heard on that dark road many years ago, my pride would be healthy and well-fed if it was just me and Jesus.

That's not to criticize George. He had a specific command from the Lord to not make his needs known. He even said others shouldn't follow His example because his was a unique calling. Most of us have a different calling - a calling to invite people to join us in the exciting adventure God has led us into.

And that's one of the "secrets" to success – listen to the Lord and obey His unique plan for you. That's not only a plan for success in building a support team but in every area of life – listen and obey.

My potential for pride is one reason the Lord led me down the "pray, trust God and invite others to participate" route of funding ministry. But the truth is, nearly 100% of Christian ministries pray, trust God and make their needs known in order to adequately accomplish what the Lord has called them to do. It is the norm, not the aberration, and I believe there is a good reason why.

I've been at this over 25 years and I have seen a not so surprising trend. Those who pray, trust God and share their needs with others are usually happier, better funded and able to be more effective than those who just pray and trust God. Probably every ministry you know of regularly makes their needs know.

But like your Momma said, "Just because everyone else does it, that doesn't make it right." We need to know, "What does the Bible say about it? Is there a Biblical model for funding ministry? Is there a Biblical precedent for asking others to financially support my work? Is it right to tell others about my needs?"

It's time to ask that four-letter question: WWJD?

What Would Jesus Do?

I was surprised when I found that Jesus had "many" financial partners in his ministry.

> *Joanna the wife of Chuza, the manager of Herod's household; Susanna; and many others. These women were helping to support them out of their own means.*
> *Luke 8:3*

Think about that. Jesus could feed thousands with a little bread and fish - and have more left over than when He started! To pay His taxes He sent Peter fishing. (Matthew 14:17) He certainly didn't need their charity. In fact, I would think that if someone had offered to support Him He would have suggested they give it to the poor.

But He took their money!

Perhaps even more amazing, their partnership was so meaningful that the Holy Spirit not only told us about it, He deliberately recorded their names. God noted, and memorialized for all eternity, donors to His ministry. Isn't that remarkable? He gave these women an opportunity to do what they could do, to be part of His mission here on earth.

Paul the apostle also had financial supporters, both individuals and churches, that enabled his ministry. Their deeds of generosity are also forever recorded in God's eternal Word.

*And when I was with you and was in need, I did not
burden anyone, for my needs were supplied by the
friends who came from Macedonia.*
2 Corinthians 11:9

*You Philippians indeed know that in the early days
of the gospel, when I left Macedonia, no church
shared with me in the matter of giving and receiv-
ing, except you alone.*
Philippians 4:15

Jesus and Paul had financial supporters.

That's nice to know but it still doesn't answer the
big question: Is it OK for us to share our needs and
invite others to invest financially in our work? Or
should we not mention it and just hope people will
figure it out and hear from God on their own?

Did Paul, the "tentmaker missionary," who made
it clear he didn't want to be a burden to others, ask
people to support his ministry? In his letter to the
Christians in Rome he tells them about his travel
plans.

*I am planning to go to Spain, and when I do, I will
stop off in Rome. And after I have enjoyed your fellowship for a little while, you can provide for my
journey.*
Romans 15:24

You can provide for my journey?!

That's bold! No hints. No veiled suggestions. He
didn't even ask. He was totally confident they
would want to do this. He wrote like he was extend-

ing them a privilege – the privilege of being part of his ministry by funding the next leg of his trip.

In the context of their culture, when he said he was coming, it also meant they were expected to feed and house him while he was there. But his expectation went beyond caring for him while he was with them. "You can take care of me while I'm there and when I'm ready to leave you can buy my plane ticket to Spain."

He didn't invite or suggest. He expected the church in Rome to participate financially in his ministry.

But what if they were in a tight financial position? What if this would put a strain on their budget? Is it right to ask people to give when they may still have needs in their own home and family?

Consider this: We know God uses support raising to challenge and stretch the faith of the support raiser. But it's easy to forget that He's also at work in the life of the donor. Supporting God's ministers is a way He challenges donors to trust Him in bigger and more profound ways.

If everything we do can be done by our own efforts, our own resources, within our own budget, how does God get any glory out of that? The glory of God lies beyond what we are able to do in our own strength.

God's goal is that both those who give and those who receive continually listen to Him and look to

Him with expectation. As givers and receivers, when we obey Him, we thrill to see His miraculous provision in surprising ways. That way the one who sows and the one who reaps can both rejoice together as the harvest is brought in. (John 4:36)

Why Do We Look To The Exceptions?

So, it is the Biblical and the historical norm to expect God to provide through His people and to let them know of the needs – in Paul's case, transportation to Spain.

In 2000 years of church history there have been a few notable exceptions but the vast majority of ministries fully inform and frequently invite donors to participate financially in their work.

Why do we look at one or two exceptions and try to make them the rule? Perhaps because, like me, we don't want our pride confronted.

Perhaps we fail to understand that we are actually cheating others if we do not give them an opportunity to be part of what God is doing through us. Perhaps we have believed the lies: Support raising is begging; making needs known is placing our trust in people; truly spiritual people don't tell anyone, they trust God.

After over a quarter of a century of raising support to enable ministry I still struggle with the old carnal nature - a.k.a. pride.

I still have to remind myself of the truths I'll share in this little book. In fact, one of the reasons I needed to write it, was as a reminder to me. You see, there are times I'm not grateful I raise support. There are times I want to "get a real job". Many times I feel people have got to be tired of hearing me share about my needs because I sure get tired of sharing them.

If you find yourself having to make your needs known to people as well as to the Lord, here are five reasons you can be grateful you raise support. I hope they will encourage you to boldly invite others to share in the privilege of ministry and reward He has invited you into.

I have tried raising money by asking for it,
and by not asking for it.
I always got more by asking for it.

- Millard Fuller -
Founder of Habitat for Humanity

In Touch with My Heart Attitudes

... when I was in Thessalonica you sent help more than once. I don't say this because I want a gift from you. Rather, I want you to receive a reward for your kindness.

Philippians 4:16, 17 NLT

A Heart Exam

When our family of five moved to Guatemala there was no email, internet, FaceTime or other amazing instant ways to stay in touch so we were left communicating with our donors the same way Paul did - through written newsletters.

One day I picked up our printed letters and it was time to fold them and insert them in those exotic airmail envelopes, with the red, white and blue trim around the outside edge. Then we had to peel and stick each address label, lick and stick the envelope, and finally lick and stick the nasty tasting Guatemalan stamps. It was a tedious process and not the kind of family night our kids looked forward to.

This particular time, our oldest son Joel, was extra vocal in his resistance. As he stuffed letter after letter he mumbled and grumbled, "So you mean if we don't send out these letters no one will support us and we can't be missionaries?"

His continual fussing had worn through whatever patience I might have had when we started the project. I decided it was time to shut down the whine factory. "That's right!" I barked. "Now stop complaining and keep stuffing!"

As soon as I said that, I heard a tiny voice in my heart ask, "Do you really believe that? Do you believe it's these newsletters that keep funds coming in for this ministry?"

It was a good question. Was I putting my trust in these newsletters or was my trust still squarely in God? Was I trusting my own efforts or was I trusting the Lord to provide for His ministry?

Support raising gives us regular opportunities to check the condition of our heart.

To be honest, I love seeing a well-crafted presentation complete with coordinated glossy brochures, colorful charts, graphs, response cards, social media releases and an interactive website. I admire the thought, creativity and artistry that's required to put something like that together. Because of that, it's easy for me to want to create a slick presentation, to creatively "package" the needs and opportunities.

And while I do think we need to make all our communication as interesting and informative as possible, I need to constantly check my heart to make sure I am depending on God - not my imagined amazing presentation - to touch the hearts of those that He wants to be part of our ministry.

God wants our trust to be squarely in Him and Him alone. If I begin to look to another source - my own efforts or other people - He has a way of quickly shutting that down. He has a way of revealing my wrong motives and re-focusing my trust on Him.

Why Waste Money on Ministry Reports?

It may seem contradictory to say, "We must fully trust God but we should still send out well-crafted reports of our ministry." If we're trusting God why waste mental energy trying to make our reports interesting? In fact, why waste time and money sending newsletters or reports at all?

A friend of mine was going through financial struggles and decided to go to his pastor for financial advice. The pastor asked him about his income and expenses.

In one column, on a white board, the pastor totaled all my friend's monthly income. In another column, he totaled his monthly expenses. The expenses were more than the income.

"There's your problem," Pastor Obvious pointed out, "Your monthly expenses are more than your monthly income. What are you going to do about it?"

My friend was a little frustrated. "Of course my bills are more than my income," he thought. "That's why I'm here! What am I going to do about it? That's what I want you to tell me!"

Realizing it was his pastor asking the question he figured he should give a respectful and spiritual answer. "What am I going to do about it? Uh, trust God?"

The pastor's response was brilliant. "Of course you're going to trust God but, what are you going to do while you're trusting God?"

We trust God and we also do something while trusting. In fact, doing something is often the way we demonstrate that we trust God.

Noah built an ark because he trusted God. The ark was a huge billboard declaring, "I believe God is going to do what He said He will do. He will flood the earth and deliver me." Noah's trust motivated his hands. Faith and hard work melded together to save him, his family and the entire human race.

David demonstrated he trusted God by finding five smooth stones. River stones couldn't defeat a giant but they became a tool God used to bring victory. Nehemiah built a wall because he trusted God to deliver and restore His people.

"Trusting God" doesn't mean we do nothing. Rather, we demonstrate we trust God by our actions.

Ministry reports can be a desperate attempt on the part of support raisers to pluck the heart strings of donors or they can be a way to demonstrate we believe God will provide all the resources necessary to complete His work. Like David's smooth stones, a newsletter is simply a tool, an earthly tool God uses to accomplish a heavenly goal.

But thoughtful ministry reports also serve another crucial purpose. Each donor is responsible to God for how they invest His resources. If they're not hearing from a missionary, they don't know what they're investing in and probably should stop supporting that work.

Ministry reports provide accountability for the support raiser – a way to let donors know how the funds they are investing are being used to advance God's kingdom.

If I see sending regular ministry reports as a necessary evil it becomes a tedious, distasteful chore. But when I remind myself that they are a chance to connect with my team and let them know what God is doing through our partnership, they become an exciting opportunity.

Love People, Use Things

Most missionaries are type A, get-the-job-done-whatever-the-cost people. They willingly make whatever sacrifice is necessary to take the hill, to vanquish the foe, to plant the flag of victory. In that zeal, it's easy to begin to see people as tools to finish the task rather than the eternal treasure of the kingdom.

We start well by loving people and using things. But with the best of intentions it's easy to morph and begin using people and loving things.

Projects take priority. The to-do list reigns supreme and checking off a task on that list equals success. But Jesus' top priority was always people - the true kingdom riches.

We value gold, jewels and gems. God uses them as pavement and building material. He values people.

In fact, He so treasures His people that He allowed His dear Son to be brutally murdered to redeem us.

I find that support raising provides a way for God to quickly get my attention if my affections begin to get out of alignment with His.

As a fallen race, we all have heart problems and need regular checkups. Because of my direct dependence upon God each day for my "daily bread," support raising keeps me alert to any dangerous heart conditions that might be developing.

I'm grateful I raise support because it forces me to regularly check my heart attitudes toward God, money and others.

What good does it do if you say you have faith but do not do things that prove you have faith? Can that kind of faith save you ....? faith that does not do things is a dead faith. .... I will prove to you I have faith by doing things.
James 2:14-18

In Touch With God

Where your treasure is, there will your heart also be.

Matthew 6:21

Stop Giving!

When I read the story in Exodus 36 it's easy to think, "Are you kidding?" The people of Israel, who were living as wandering nomads in a wilderness, were asked to donate to build a sanctuary. They gave so much that Moses commanded them to stop giving.

I can't imagine, and I've certainly never heard of, a church or Christian ministry saying, "Stop! Stop giving. We have more than we need."

Surely God is not short of funds but it seems most of his ministers and ministries always are. I've sometimes wondered why.

God is certainly capable of lavishing His people with more than enough. Every church and Christian ministry could have stores of funds waiting in the bank, ready to pull out and help meet any need that arises.

"You need $500 to help with your medical expenses? No problem. Where do we send the check?"

"You need $2 billion to provide clean water for all of Haiti? No problem. Where do we send the check?"

Wouldn't that be awesome? I think so, but obviously, God doesn't.

As I've thought about it, I believe one reason He keeps the funds tight, at least in my case, is that it keeps me tight with Him. It keeps me daily dependent. I can't run very far ahead of Him. And He seems to like walking close by my side every day.

It seems He has always preferred walking closely with His people day by day.

When God delivered the Israelites from Egypt he could have just given Moses a map like the one in the back of your Bible. It was a simple route, a straight shot, no way to get lost.

"Here Moses. Look at the map on page 5006. You're here. I'll meet you at Kadesh – that's D5 on the map. I'll see you there in a month."

But He chose to accompany them day and night for what turned out to be a very long 40-year trip. They couldn't get impatient and run ahead or fall behind. Each day they had to look to Him to provide manna - their daily bread - and to provide guidance. If the cloud moved, they moved. If the cloud stayed, they stayed.

In the same way, support raising keeps me regularly looking to God. I'm dependent upon Him for my "daily bread."

If I want to get involved in some project, I can only move ahead if He provides the necessary funds. If the funds aren't there I can't move. And I've found that His lack of provision is just as directional as His provision. And, that delays are often not denials, but merely a matter of synchronizing me with His perfect timing.

The Danger of Too Much

Some years ago, a friend put me in touch with a rather wealthy couple who had a vision. He thought I might be able to help them fulfill their dream. As we talked, it became obvious that their idea was totally impractical.

It was one of those things that sounds good to a North American who does not understand the culture, mindset or limitations of the poor in Central

America. A great idea that had no possibility of success.

As I tried to explain why this wouldn't work and offer suggestions of more practical ways they could help, it quickly became obvious they would not be persuaded. They were on a mission from God.

Their vision was never realized but they did manage to waste many hours of my time and the time of others plus thousands of dollars before they went on to their next mission from God.

That experience produced a sense of gratitude in me for my limited resources. I realized, when you have an abundance of cash it's easy to casually waste it on "good ideas" that aren't God ideas. And I don't want the accountability before God that comes with that.

When running on a tight budget we are much more aware of our need for God's guidance. We have less margin for error. That means I not only have to hear from God but I also know how important it is to listen to the wisdom of others.

Finally, the validity of your idea has to be confirmed by God touching donors' hearts to get on board and make it possible. If He doesn't do it, it won't happen.

That can be a frustrating place to live, but it's also a safe place - especially for those of us who can generate a thousand good ideas a day. Support raising keeps me listening to the Lord, unable to run too far ahead because I'm on a short leash. But it's precious to remember, the fact that the leash is short also means He is always close to me.

A Constant Reminder

Because I raise support I am constantly aware of my dependence upon the Lord. If God doesn't touch people's hearts and if those people don't obey, I could have no income, no paycheck, no way to pay bills or provide for my family.

That much direct and constant dependence upon the Lord can be challenging. I've talked with support raisers who are considering jettisoning their call and getting "a real job" just to have some financial security. But, in reality, the guy who receives a pay check every week is just as dependent upon the Lord's faithfulness as the support raiser.

I became keenly aware of this when a friend, who worked almost 30 years for a huge international corporation, suddenly lost his job.

Previously he had great benefits and knew that every week there would be a hefty paycheck coming his way. He thought he was safely coasting toward a secure retirement.

Previously it was easy to view his job, his company and his own hard work as his source and provider. When that changed overnight, he realized he had always been just as dependent on God as I was.

It just wasn't as evident in his situation as it was in mine.

The guy who has "a real job" has to regularly remind himself that his job and the company are not his source.

In my case, I can never forget it because each donation reminds me that God touched someone's heart and that someone obeyed the Lord's prompting to give. I'm supported by God's grace and the obedience of His people.

This constant awareness of my dependence upon the Lord is both a blessing and a bane - a blessing to my spiritual life but a bane to my carnal nature.

It can be tempting to look for something more steady, more predictable, more secure. But when I'm anxious about my income I know I have shifted my focus off my true Provider.

I recently read a story about Katherine von Bora - the wife of the reformer, Martin Luther. Normally Martin was a cheerful fellow but at times the stress became overwhelming.

During one of those difficult periods Katherine put on a black mourning dress and met Martin at the door.

"Who died?" Martin asked. Katherine explained that God had died.

Of course Martin rebuked her for her foolishness asking where she got such a silly idea. She replied, "God must be dead or Doctor Luther would not be so sorrowful." Her rebuke hit home and Luther snapped out of his depression.

What a lesson to support raisers. Unless God's dead I don't need to worry. The Boss is well, the family business is booming and my position in the company is as secure as His promises.

I'm grateful I raise support because it keeps me aware of my constant dependence on God.

We think you ought to know about the trouble we went through .... as a result, we stopped relying on ourselves and learned to rely only on God ... And you are helping us by praying for us.
2 Corinthians 1:8-11

In Touch
With Wonderful People

A friend is always loyal, and a brother is born to help in time of need.

Proverbs 17:17 NLT

Who Is Rescuing Whom?

We were back in the U.S. visiting a small church that had a missionary family as guest speakers. The father told us how he heard a call from God to go to Native Americans and went.

It was obvious he was very proud of the fact that they didn't ask anybody for help. They didn't talk with a church, they didn't wait to build a financial or prayer support team. They were "trusting God." So they sold everything and drove across country and onto a reservation.

The next 20 minutes he told a harrowing story of getting lost in a blizzard on the first day. Their car got stuck in the snow on an unmarked road. They ran out of gas with nothing and no one in sight.

They were on the brink of freezing to death in their car when a pick-up truck with a Native American family came by. There was nowhere to take them. There was no one to call for help. They were in the middle of a deadly blizzard.

The Native American family did the only thing they could do - they invited them into the truck and took them to their home. What a miracle! God had saved His missionaries.

But the "miracle" didn't stop there. God continued to provide. The father told how this Native American family, that had so little themselves, shared their limited food for the next three weeks.

Finally, the blizzard stopped and the snow melted enough for them to get out of the house.

About this time, my daughter, who was captivated by their story, leaned over and whispered to me, "Wow, Dad. We never had to go through anything like that."

I whispered back, "They might not have had to go through it either if they had talked with other people, gotten some wise counsel, enlisted people to pray for them and done a little research before they drove off on their own."

This guy reminded me of the Lone Ranger setting off to singlehandedly save Tonto. But this presumptuous Lone Ranger, and his hapless family, ended up being rescued by those they went to save.

He was proud of the fact that they were trusting God. Unlike other missionaries they didn't need people. They were following the Lord's command and trusting He would provide for them.

But, in reality, he did need people. In reality he had a prayer and support team. He just found his prayer and support team in a rather inconsiderate way.

What was that Native American family supposed to do when they found this car full of goofy white folks stranded in a blizzard? You either take them home with you now or you chip their frozen bodies out of the car in a few weeks when the snow melts.

The Native American family was forced to become an involuntary support team for these missionaries. I'm willing to bet the host family was also a prayer team - praying regularly it would quit snowing so they could get these moochers out of their home.

God never designed us to be lone rangers. In fact, he says, "Two are better than one ... Pity the man who is alone because if he stumbles he has no one to help him up." (Ecclesiastes 4:9-10)

I'm grateful I raise support because it puts a positive pressure on me to reach out and connect with others. It forces me to do something very wonderful - stay in touch with friends who encourage me and who I can encourage.

A Lost Treasure

There is no way the Lone Ranger mentioned above could realize the treasure he was sacrificing by going it alone - the priceless treasure of friends and co-laborers.

Many on our support team are families we would have never met if we were not raising support. Perhaps we met them while sharing at a church. Perhaps a mutual friend introduced us. Whatever brought us together, it was the bond that we formed by working together that kept us together.

They are part of our lives and we are part of theirs. We keep up with them, watch their families grow, rejoice with them and occasionally cry with them - just like they do with us.

These folks have become part of our family. Some have visited us on the field and stayed in our home. We have stayed in many of their homes. We have precious memories of being taken to a circus or a professional baseball game by these wonderful members of our mission team.

Our support family is scattered across the country. In fact, there are some we have never met in person. But we have exchanged letters, pictures and prayers during good times and rough times.

When Jana and I sit to pray together each morning, we also pray for our support team members by name. Every time I write them I can't help but rehearse in my mind the memories of these folks who are such an important part of our ministry. But it's also their ministry.

It couldn't happen without their involvement, without their partnership.

Sadly, "The Lone Ranger" mentality short-circuits others from sharing in the benefit and blessing of the work.

Many don't feel called or able to do what the missionary does but, like the women who supported Jesus, through giving they can share in the joy and reward. They can do what they've been called to do in missions.

If God has called you to an effective and exciting work, why wouldn't you invite others to participate and share with you in it?

I'm reminded of the story of Joshua fighting the Amalekites in Exodus 17. As long as Moses held up his rod, Joshua won the battle.

But Moses' arms quickly grew tired. As soon as he lowered his arms, Joshua started losing. Aaron and Hur came to the rescue and held Moses' tired arms up until the Israelites declared victory.

Joshua swung the sword but he couldn't have won without the help of Moses, who couldn't have done it without the support of Aaron and Hur. All four men were equally important to winning the victory. They were all essential members of the team.

If You Want To Go Far ...

I may be on the front line swinging the sword but I, and every CTEN missionary, depend upon a prayer and financial support team, as well as the administrative home staff of CTEN. All are essential members of the team driving back the darkness and making the name of Jesus known in the nations.

An African proverb says, "If you want to go fast, go alone. If you want to go far, go with others." We are in this for the long haul – to go far. We have been called to make disciples, not just converts.

We're in this to win. We win when we go with others.

I'm grateful I raise support because it enables me to connect with many wonderful people and regularly stay in touch with them as more than friends, but as members of the family and partners in our mutual ministry.

Every time I think of you, I give thanks to my God.
Whenever I pray, I make my requests for all of you with
joy, for you have been my partners in spreading the
Good News about Christ from the time you first heard
it until now.
Philippians 1:3-5 NLT

REASON 4

In Touch
With Miracles From God

So don't worry about these things, saying, "What will we eat? What will we drink? What will we wear?" These things dominate the thoughts of unbelievers, but your heavenly Father already knows all your needs.

Matthew 6:31, 32

What? Me Worry?

I tend to be very practical when I read Scripture. Sometimes that leads to rather irreverent outcomes. I know I'm supposed to rejoice that "his eye is on the sparrow". But when I read Matthew 10:29 - not a single sparrow can fall to the ground without your Father knowing it - I remember pale, limp, little bird-bodies I've seen baking in the sun covered with a hoard of hungry ants.

It doesn't comfort me to know that God's aware of that sparrow. If I fall to the pavement I want to believe He's going to rescue me, not just sit back and watch me become a bug banquet.

I'm grateful I raise support because it has provided countless opportunities for God to bail me out. I've experienced His glorious care both in big areas and small ones. I've seen that He's not just aware of my needs but He takes great delight in rescuing me in amazing and miraculous ways.

My wife, three kids and I were driving through Southern Mexico on our way back to the United States. We had seen nothing but cactus and wasteland for what seemed like hours when something under the hood of our old Suburban exploded. That was followed by a violent, pulsating hissing.

Because I'm quite intuitive when it comes to mechanical things I was instantly able to ascertain, "Something's wrong."

A few hundred yards ahead I could see a place to pull off the road. When I stopped, I noticed a small locked shed and five Mexican men relaxing under a tin roof lean-to that provided some protection from the scorching sun. There was no one and nothing else around.

I popped the hood of the Suburban - not because I had any idea of what to look for but because that's what guys do to let everyone know they've got things under control.

The heat from under the hood hit me like a furnace. I looked around and saw a spark plug cable hanging loose.

Hmmm. That doesn't look right. I reached for it to see if I could figure out where it was supposed to go. Dumb idea! Wow, it was hot!

I jumped back and let out a yell. (It doesn't take me long to look at a hot spark plug wire.) My antics provided some entertainment for my very interested group of Mexican spectators.

I walked over and asked if they had any idea where I could find a mechanic. A fellow swaying slowly in a hammock casually raised a finger to indicate that he was the guy I was looking for.

Really?

We are in the middle of nowhere. I have no idea what these guys are doing here. There is nothing around but this lean-to shelter and a locked 10x10 shed. This is definitely not a mechanic shop but here is a mechanic - with tools!

He meandered over and poked around under the hood. I became majorly alarmed when he pointed out the problem. One of my spark plugs had blown apart. I didn't even know they could do that!

The top of the plug was stuck in the rubber cup at the end of the spark plug wire. No problem. But the lower half of the plug was still securely screwed into the engine block. Big problem. To me it looked hopeless.

The engine was way too hot to touch and even if we could, there was no way to get that plug out of the block. We had no electricity, no drill or special-ty tools and these guys didn't even have a car to go get anything we needed. It was literally just the five of them sitting in the shade in the middle of no-where.

But my new amigo didn't seem the least bit wor-ried. Of course, he had no reason to worry. It was me, my wife and three kids that were stuck in the desert, in the blistering sun, with no way to get our vehicle fixed.

He suggested that I sit in the car and let him get to work. Why not? I had no idea how to help.

After about 20 minutes he walked up to me hold-ing the end of the plug he had retrieved from the engine block.

I couldn't believe it! Then I wished I had stayed with him to see how he accomplished this miracle, especially since the engine was still hotter than a habanero.

But I still needed a replacement plug. I asked if he knew where I could get a new spark plug. At least I asked something like that since I wasn't positive how to say "spark plug" in Spanish. "El spark-o plug-o?"

"Si," and he signaled me to follow him. We walked back toward his buddies and he began kicking the dust. I couldn't believe it. There were several old spark plugs lying in the dirt.

He picked one up. He dusted it off and we headed back to the car. Within a few minutes we cranked it up and everything ran great.

Then it dawned on me, it was time to "pay the piper". We were in the middle of nowhere. This guy just performed a total miracle and saved my whole family. He can charge whatever outrageous amount he wants and I'll have to pay it.

"How much do I owe you?" I asked.

When he answered, I thought my Spanish was failing me. I couldn't believe what I heard so I asked, "Are you serious?"

Yes, he was serious. All he wanted was that we give him something to drink.

We had some boxed drinks for the kids in an ice chest in the car. We gave him a couple of juices and some chocolate milk. He happily returned to his hammock and we were on our way - in stunned amazement, convinced that we had just had an angelic mechanic encounter.

His Pre-Vision Prompts His Provision

In addition to God taking care of us through miraculous stories such as that we have seen the Lord provide amazing sums of money at crucial times. At one point it became comical how directly He provided for us. If we had a large gift come in we knew an unexpected expense was coming.

Time after time that is exactly what happened - a car repair, a ministry need, something.

One month we received an unexpected gift of $300. My wife and I smiled at each other. "I wonder what this is for?"

Sure enough, we had a surprise water bill for $300. Yes, $300 for water, for one month!

The government water company admitted it was their fault. Their meter had broken. But now they had fixed it and we needed to pay the full bill.

To make sure I understood correctly, I repeated, "Your meter was broken and says we used more water than we could have possibly used. Correct?"

"Si, amigo, that's correct. But now the meter is fixed so you need to pay the bill or we will cut off your water." It all made perfect sense to them.

Apparently, God understands how bureaucrats think and graciously provided ahead of time.

I'm grateful I raise support because it allows me to see God regularly provide for me, my family and our ministry in miraculous ways.

And this same God who takes care of me will supply all your needs from his glorious riches, which have been given to us in Christ Jesus.
Philippians 4:19 NLT

In Touch
With God's Blessings
For Others

Remember this—a farmer who plants only a few seeds will get a small crop. But the one who plants generously will get a generous crop. You must each decide in your heart how much to give. And don't give reluctantly or in response to pressure.

"For God loves a person who gives cheerfully." And God will generously provide all you need. Then you will always have everything you need and plenty left over to share with others.

2 Corinthians 9:6-8 NLT

No Seed Too Tiny

The first time I opened a package of carrot seeds I thought I'd been ripped off. I tore open the small envelope and it was filled with dust - or so I thought. Carrot seeds are tiny.

I was reminded of those seeds when a friend wrote to say she wanted to support our ministry but that she didn't have much money and knew that her little gift wouldn't make a difference.

In 2 Corinthians 9, our financial gifts are compared to seed, so I asked her, "How big does a seed have to be before it's worth planting?"

One of our financial partners is a widow and former missionary herself. For years she has faithfully sown $2.00 a month into our ministry. As a former missionary, she knows that it's not the size of the seed that matters. Even the tiniest of seeds can produce a harvest - but only if it's planted.

And that is one of the most glorious things about raising support – it provides a way for everyone to be involved in the global harvest.

No one is too poor to sow seed into the harvest of the nations. Because it's not the size of the seed that matters but that you are doing what you are able to do.

The one who gives $2.00 and the one who gives $2,000 both share in the harvest. Each is a member of the team that enables a missionary to go and make disciples of all nations.

When Jesus stood at the temple and watched what people gave, He didn't condemn the large donors. But He only commended the one who gave sacrificially, the one who gave more than she could afford. (Mark 12:43)

Salvation is free but delivering it to "every nation, every tribe and every tongue" is costly. Thank God for those who can invest large amounts in missions. They are essential members of the world harvest team.

But just as much a part of the team are those who are only able to invest small amounts. Jesus commended the widow because she did what she could - she gave out of her need. (Mark 12:41-44)

Whether we are able to give a large amount or a small amount, by investing in missions we get in on a fraction of the action.

Why You Can't Give to Missions

I was giving online to a missionary when a strange thought occurred to me, "I'm not really giving anything here. In fact, I can't give to missions or missionaries."

A gift implies we get nothing in return. But Scripture makes it clear that when we give to the Lord,

He notices and "that person will certainly not lose their reward." (Matthew 10:42)

Instead of giving to missions, I was investing. And I was investing in a sure thing. It had God's guarantee of return.

The best financial advice ever given came from Jesus Himself. He didn't suggest pouring cash into real estate or stocks, bonds or treasury notes. He said, "Store up treasure in heaven." (Matthew 6:20)

Investing in missions is one way we store up treasure in heaven where it is safe from theft, economic downturn or loss. It's a guaranteed safe investment that's good for eternity. What other investment can make that promise?

The Joy of Personal Involvement

I was talking with a long-time partner of our ministry. Bill had visited us on the field and he and his wife Margie had adopted our family into theirs. At one point, I tried to express how much their friendship and partnership meant to us.

But he stopped me short. "Please don't thank me," he said. "I want to thank you that I get to be part of your ministry. We are privileged to invest where we know how our funds are being used, where we know the people we are giving to and can actually meet the people we are helping."

I was humbled and surprised by his response. But a few years later I got to experience first-hand what he was talking about.

When I first became aware of the horror of human trafficking I wanted to do something. I wanted to give to a ministry that was fighting this demon. But this was before it became a well-publicized tragedy that many ministries were combatting.

I tried to find someone involved in rescuing the victims of slavery. I knew missionaries from around the globe but couldn't find a single person who even knew someone who was involved in that ministry.

We now have several Commission To Every Nation missionaries involved in combatting human trafficking but back then, after all my searching, all I could find was one large ministry that was involved.

I did my research (I checked them out www.CharityNavigator.org and www.ecfa.org) and found this big ministry was doing a magnificent job, so I started sending funds their way.

It was good to know I was doing something but I wished I could have found an individual or small organization that I could have partnered with in a more personal way.

I would have preferred to be able to talk with them, ask if there was anything else I could do. I wanted to know the names of the workers and the people I was helping.

The large organization was doing a great job and worthy of support but, for me, I wanted to feel more personally involved, closer to the problem and the solution.

It was then that I realized what Bill meant when he said he valued being part of our family and part of our team. He knew us. He heard from us. If he had questions, we welcomed a call from this friend and partner.

I thank God for huge organizations. Their vast resources sometimes enable them to do things that individuals and smaller operations can't. Most are doing wonderful things for God's kingdom and I occasionally send funds to them. But, when I'm able, I like to be involved at a more personal level.

Six Reasons I Prefer Investing In Individuals

1. Connection

When I support an individual missionary I can call them, email them, connect with them just to say, "Hello. How are you? I'm praying for you."

When they write and say "Thank you," I know I'm not just an unknown name on a huge mailing list. We become friends working together to accomplish an important kingdom endeavor.

2. Impact

If I send $100 gift to a multi-million-dollar ministry, it's just a tiny drop in the huge bucket of donations they'll need to operate that month.

But $100 is a large amount for me to give and when I give it to an individual missionary I know it's a significant gift for them to receive.

Percentage-wise my gift does much more to help an individual missionary than a huge agency with gigantic monthly budget requirements.

3. Accountability

I can go see first-hand the missionaries I'm supporting and I'm welcomed as a friend. I can meet their co-workers, the people they serve and the people that my gift helps. I can call or email and ask how things are going, what they're doing, what their needs are and what their goals are.

And I know my call or visit is viewed as an encouragement from an interested friend rather than a nuisance from a nosey, anonymous donor.

4. Return on Investment

Most individual missionaries I know are doing amazing things on a shoestring budget. They miraculously stretch every dime and every dollar because every dime and every dollar is precious. They have to learn to do more with less. That means even a small gift makes a big difference.

5. Limited Contacts

I know that an individual missionary's circle of potential donors is tiny compared to a nation-wide ministry that can run television ads, magazine ads and even set up displays at conferences to recruit new donors.

An individual missionary does not have the time nor funds to reach thousands of potential donors. He is limited to friends, family and friends of friends.

And, his circle of potential donors decreases as he loses touch with people due to being "out of sight and out of mind" serving in his target country.

6. Personal Experience

Finally, I prefer to support individual missionaries because I am one. I know how much each and every donor on our support team means to us. I've seen the depth of impact an individual or a family can have when empowered by God.

Whether sending to an individual missionary or a huge ministry, when we invest in missions we buy into God's economy of blessing.

We store up treasure in heaven and we make an eternal impact here on earth.

I'm grateful I raise support because this ministry allows everyone, regardless of their financial status, to become personally involved in missions and tap into the harvest God promises to those who sow into the kingdom.

If you receive a prophet as one who speaks for God, you will be given the same reward as a prophet.
And if you receive righteous people because of their righteousness, you will be given a reward like theirs.
And if you give even a cup of cold water to one of the least of my followers, you will surely be rewarded.
Matthew 10:41, 42 NL

How Much Money Should A Missionary Raise?

I Didn't Have Anything To Give

One of our CTEN missionaries always seemed underfunded. I knew what it took to live in the country where he served and I couldn't figure out how he managed to live on the little bit of monthly support he had.

One day we were talking and he explained why he didn't put more effort into building a bigger support team. "A lot of time I run out of money before I run out of month. I may not have any food in the house for a couple of days but I'm a little overweight anyway so I just see it as a chance to fast."

I suggested that additional funds would enable him to extend his ministry and then he could voluntarily fast. We agreed it would be a good idea to increase his level of support and we then changed the subject, both knowing he wasn't going to do anything about it.

A few months later this missionary contacted me to say he was going to focus on increasing his monthly support. I was surprised and asked to hear his story.

"It was the end of the month. I had absolutely no food in my house when three boys from the neighborhood knocked at my gate.

'Our mother sent us to ask if you could give us some food. We don't have any and we're hungry.'

"I was devastated. I didn't have a thing to give them but I knew they couldn't understand that. In their minds, all Americans are rich and my size clearly shows I don't miss many meals.

"I knew they would think I was lying and that I just didn't want to help them. It broke my heart to have to send them away empty-handed but I literally didn't have anything to give them.

"Now I realize I need to raise additional funds so I'll never have to say, 'I can't help you. I have nothing to give.'"

While this story is sad, it's not uncommon. In response to the question, "How much money should a missionary raise?" many are content with "Enough to get by."

But God hasn't called us to "get by." He has called us to minister, to make a difference, to impact those around us. That takes resources.

But how much is enough?

The Answer

How much money should a missionary raise? Enough to be effective.

God has called us to effectively minister in His name, not to just get by. Raise enough that you can afford the tools that will make you effective. Raise enough that you can stay healthy and as safe as reasonably possible.

If you have a family, raise enough that your spouse and children don't suffer because you are content to just get by.

God is not broke and does not run the universe on a shoestring budget. Often, we "have not because we ask not." We fail to ask God because we think He is pleased with us just getting by.

But notice that when Jesus fed the thousands there was an abundance of leftovers. Our God is not a "just enough to get by" God. He wants to provide plenty so we have more than enough to share with others.

Like my friend at the start of this section, most of us would rather fast three days a month than talk to people about our needs. We'd rather "get by."

But, God has not called us simply to live in a place, survive. He has called us to effectively represent His kingdom and give ourselves and our resources to those we serve.

Effectiveness requires having enough "loaves and fishes" to feed ourselves and have enough to share with others.

How Should We Then Live?

The Tension: Early Burn-out or Out-of-Touch?

A tension some missionaries struggle with is, "At what economic level should I live?"

Do I live exactly like those I'm ministering to?

Do I try to maintain a North American lifestyle?

Or should my standard of living be somewhere in between?

Of course, some missionaries have no choice based upon their location. An American serving in Japan might actually find the US a step-down after serving in Japan. A Canadian living in a remote Brazilian jungle probably doesn't have to decide whether he should have cable TV or not.

But for most missionaries, a tension exists as to how "incarnational" they should be – how much they should live like those they ministry to and with.

I heard a missionary to Africa explain that his original plan was for him and his family to move and live full-time in the village with the people they were translating the Bible for. This meant frequent battles with malaria and other tropical diseases. It meant hours a day were spent just meeting the basic necessities of life – gathering firewood, water, cooking and other essential chores necessary for survival. It meant no electricity so all translation work was done by hand without the help of powerful computer translation tools.

Eventually some of the tribe's leaders came and suggested he should live with them a few months and then go back to the capital city for a few months to work on the translation. They realized they were years away from ever seeing the Bible in their language at the slow rate of progress that village life necessitated.

He pointed out that, while it looks nice in the textbooks to say a missionary should "move into the neighborhood" and live like those he is ministering to, it can also mean less effectiveness, burn-out, and/or an early retirement due to physical and mental health issues.

But Can I Relate If I Live Differently?

If a missionary serves among the poor, a natural concern is the ability to minister effectively if the missionary lives at a different location and/or economic level than those they serve.

Another missionary from Africa writes, "My experience has been that it's not the standard of living that causes relational issues. Rather, it is a matter of a humble or a proud heart. I've seen people who make twenty times the local wage who connect deeply with the poor because they do not see themselves as better than those they serve. And, I've seen those who have just a little bit more than average who lord it over those they work with.

"I've never heard anyone claim a middle-class North American shouldn't even try to minister to the poor because it would be futile. I don't know why we think economic disparity raises an insurmountable wall as soon as we leave the US or Canada."

Obviously, I'm not advocating missionaries live an opulent lifestyle. Like all Christians, if our lifestyle is drawing attention to ourselves that should serve as a red flag for us to reevaluate our eternal priorities.

I only include this discussion because there are voices that say a "real missionary" must live with and live like those they serve. That sounds good on paper but in reality, it may lead to a shorter-than-necessary missionary career and may not increase your effectiveness.

The answer? Every missionary must hear from the Lord as to how they should live. After all, it is to your own master you will ultimately give account (Romans 14:4).

God will show you how, in your unique situation, to balance the concerns of effectiveness, emotional and physical health with the concern of incarnationally relating to those you serve.

You need to listen and follow the Lord's guidance.

You also need to be careful you do not judge others who might have been directed to live differently than you.

Finally, husbands, you need to listen to your wives.

An unmarried man can spend his time doing the Lord's work and thinking how to please him. But a married man has to think about his earthly responsibilities and how to please his wife. His interests are divided.
1 Corinthians 7:32-34

Conclusion

Give, and you will receive. Your gift will return to you in full-- pressed down, shaken together to make room for more, running over, and poured into your lap. The amount you give will determine the amount you get back.

Luke 6:38 NLT

Fearless Faith

I f you're a support raiser, I hope you are also a support giver. As you give to others, the Lord has promised to give to you.

I've observed that an attitude of open-handedness on my part promotes an open-handedness on God's part toward me. If I am tight-fisted, the Lord responds similarly toward me.

Be fearless in your giving. Don't limit it to what you can do comfortably. As long as we operate within our own comfort boundaries there is no faith involved.

God wants us to learn total dependence on Him. Only there do we discover the joy and thrill of giving.

Step out. Trust Him. Let Him use you in ever increasing measure – giving more, serving more, loving more. Be fearless in your faith.

My piece may seem small
In the plans of God's heart,
But the picture's not finished
Till I do my part.

- Richard Malm

Notes and Thoughts

God is most glorified
when He uses the least qualified.

- Richard Malm -

ABOUT THE AUTHOR

Richard Malm is founder of
Commission To Every Nation and
Commission Ministers Network.
He has raised his support to enable his ministry
with both organizations since 1990.
He is a pastor, missionary, Christian educator,
parent, grandparent and husband
to Jana for over 40 years.

You can connect with him
at
RickMalm@cten.org

Commission To Every Nation
www.cten.org
Commission Ministers Network
www.CMNetwork.org
or
www.RickMalm.com

MORE FROM RICK

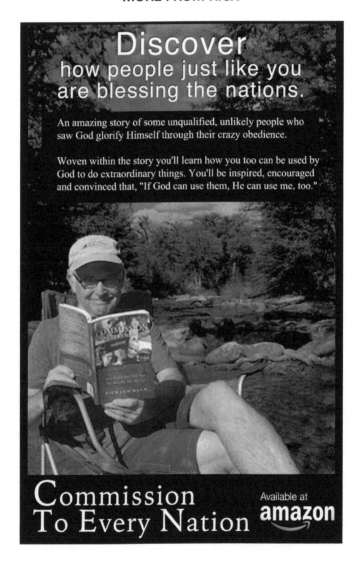

Commission To Every Nation
How People Just Like You Are Blessing the Nations

Have you ever felt unqualified to do something for God?

You're not alone. Richard Malm's pastor actually told him, "You're the most unlikely candidate for ministry I've ever met." Ouch!

But when Rick and his family moved to war-torn Guatemala, God engineered a thrilling, atypical path to founding an agency that has sent thousands of Christians into over 60 nations.

Commission To Every Nation is more than just the story of one man's reluctant journey to begin an international missions organization. It's the story of how God uses unqualified ordinary people to accomplish extraordinary results for His glory.

What others are saying:

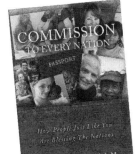

- I couldn't put it down!!
- Excellent! Loved it.
- Such an encouragement!
- I got up at 3am to finish it.
- We're reading CTEN in our fellowship group. Really good!
- This book is a must read, especially for those of us who have felt horribly unqualified to ever be used by God.
- It so grabbed my attention that I ended up finishing it in just a few hours – and marked it all up.

Order at:
www.bit.ly/ricksbooks

Spare the Rod
Five Times You Should Not Spank Your Child

Isn't spanking a barbaric form of discipline in our modern society? Doesn't spanking teach children that violence is an appropriate way to solve problems?

There is no shortage of critics when it comes to the topic of spanking but is it possible that spanking, when done within Biblical guidelines, is actually a controlled act of love that helps a child escape slavery to his own selfishness, unrestrained emotions and unbridled self-will?

Spare the Rod looks at five times it's not appropriate to spank our children. But, while doing so, it also provides guidelines for when it is appropriate and examines the heart attitude with which parents should approach it.

Perfected Praise
Leading Children Into Meaningful Worship

Now in its second printing, *Perfected Praise* will help you understand the heart of the Father toward children. It gives workable ideas to help you lead your little ones into meaningful worship.

I Like Flowers

A fun book for parent and child. Rick wrote *I Like Flowers* to share with his grandchildren. But now you and your child can enjoy this colorful, visual treat filled with images of flowers, most taken by Rick on his travels to over 50 nations.

You and your child will enjoy exploring again and again the vibrantly colored flowers and leaves, cactus and trees - while carried along with fun verse, simple rhyme and twists of humor.

27909768R00046

Made in the USA
Columbia, SC
04 October 2018